I0435016

CHILDREN MIGRATING FROM CENTRAL AMERICA: SOLVING A HUMANITARIAN CRISIS

HEARING

BEFORE THE

SUBCOMMITTEE ON THE WESTERN HEMISPHERE

OF THE

COMMITTEE ON FOREIGN AFFAIRS HOUSE OF REPRESENTATIVES

ONE HUNDRED THIRTEENTH CONGRESS

SECOND SESSION

JUNE 25, 2014

Serial No. 113–182

Printed for the use of the Committee on Foreign Affairs

Available via the World Wide Web: http://www.foreignaffairs.house.gov/ or http://www.gpo.gov/fdsys/

U.S. GOVERNMENT PRINTING OFFICE

88–460PDF   WASHINGTON : 2014

For sale by the Superintendent of Documents, U.S. Government Printing Office
Internet: bookstore.gpo.gov   Phone: toll free (866) 512–1800; DC area (202) 512–1800
Fax: (202) 512–2104   Mail: Stop IDCC, Washington, DC 20402–0001

CONTENTS

CHILDREN MIGRATING FROM CENTRAL AMERICA: SOLVING A HUMANITARIAN CRISIS

WEDNESDAY, JUNE 25, 2014

House of Representatives,
Subcommittee on the Western Hemisphere,
Committee on Foreign Affairs,
Washington, DC.

The subcommittee met, pursuant to notice, at 2 o'clock p.m., in room 2255 Rayburn House Office Building, Hon. Matt Salmon (chairman of the subcommittee) presiding.

Mr. Salmon. Quorum being present, the subcommittee will come to order and I will start by recognizing myself and Ranking Member Albio Sires to present our opening statements.

Without objection the members of the subcommittee can submit their opening remarks for the record and now I yield myself as much time as I might consume.

Good afternoon and thank you all for joining us today in convening this hearing on the humanitarian crisis that has been unfolding as a result of thousands of unoccupied children showing up at our border.

President Obama's political spin team and the White House are calling this a humanitarian situation. I visited a location where these children are being held in Nogales, Arizona. I saw children as young as four essentially warehoused and I can tell you it is not a situation. It is a crisis.

Not only have relevant agencies been overwhelmed, but our national security has been put at risk as the border security resources have been diverted to deal with the crisis. Virtually all of the 140 volunteers from the Customs and Border Patrol that are at this facility are volunteers who have basically left the border to take care of these children. In the last 8 months, over 47,000 unaccompanied minors have been apprehended at our border.

In the first part of this fiscal year, Border Patrol has seen a 700 percent increase in children coming from El Salvador alone and illegally, 930 percent increase in children coming from Guatemala, and a 1,200 percent in children coming illegally from Honduras, compared to all of 2009.

When I toured the warehouses in Nogales, I couldn't help but ask how many children didn't make it, how many became ill, were sold into prostitution, or were murdered and never made it to the border.

Since the magnitude of this crisis began hitting the airwaves, we have heard the administration scramble to describe all the push and the pull factors all of which are indeed contributing factors.

What is missing from the administration is a clear statement repudiating the President's own declaration in the Rose Garden back in 2012 the he would no longer enforce elements of our immigration laws, which has been the primary impetus for the massive increase in unaccompanied minors arriving illegally on our doorstep.

President Obama's decision to flout U.S. immigration law spread like wildfire through the region and very clearly prompted mothers and fathers in Central America to do the unthinkable—send their children on a dangerous voyage at the mercy of human traffic smugglers and criminals.

These children were lured by rumors that they would receive permisos at the border allowing them to stay, rumors originating with the President's own deferred action directive.

The fact is President Obama's unwillingness to enforce immigration law and secure our borders not only impacts the security of U.S. citizens, but has had the immoral effect of incentivizing young vulnerable children to risk their lives and suffer untold indignities rather than stay with their families where they belong.

Encouraging children to make a dangerous trek and then warehousing them away from their families is definitely not compassionate. The right and moral thing to do is reunite these children with their families in their home countries while helping those countries create conditions for security and opportunity, and I think we have a responsibility to work with those countries to get that done.

But the first step has to be taken by this administration. It is for President Obama to make a public appearance, to walk back his continued flouting of U.S. immigration and border security policy and tell the world that the United States will protect its borders while discouraging families from risking their lives and the lives of their children unnecessarily.

Press releases and letters to regional heads of state are not going to be sufficient. Public diplomacy efforts have got to be robust. The President must own his substantial role in creating this crisis.

It is the morally correct thing to do and I really hope he will. Second, we have got to take immediate steps to send those children to their country of origin to be reunited with their families.

Failure to act quickly and return these kids is going to cause even more children to risk the perilous trip north. Right now they are paying about $5,000 to $8,000 apiece.

Think of how much that represents of a person's income that lives in Honduras or El Salvador. It probably represents an entire year for them. And if they are seeing, by our actions, that those efforts are going to be fruitless and that is going to be a waste of money, it is going to stop.

Following these immediate steps we have to look at the conditions in our hemisphere that create this kind of abject desperation that would drive a parent to send their small children far away from home in search of a better life.

We spend time on this subcommittee looking at the insecurity that plagues Central America, the criminality fused by transnational criminal organizations and gangs and the lack of economic opportunity that is made worse by these realities.

I convened this hearing today because I want to work with State and USAID to find better and more effective ways to help the countries of Central America to combat this scourge of criminality and empower economic growth and opportunity.

The dangerous level of criminality is absolutely a contributing factor to the shocking uptick in unaccompanied minors making this dangerous trip to escape the growing violence in the Northern Triangle. Honduras has the highest murder rate in the world with El Salvador and Guatemala ranked fourth and fifth.

Reports from Honduras and El Salvador reveal that children are increasingly forced to participate in gang and criminal activities. We need to take a hard look at specific CARSI programs to evaluate if they have been truly effective at combating the scourge of narcotics trafficking and criminal enterprises.

Mexico is affected by the growing violence in Central America just as we are. We have got to find ways to get Mexico to take a bigger role in helping Central American nations in partnership with the United States, and to that end I would like to see an itemized accounting of the types of USAID programs being employed in the region and an honest assessment of whether or not they are working. This is a crisis.

In addition, I would like to convey my frustration that over the last 18 months, we have conducted several hearings on the region and specifically the challenges and opportunities facing the Western Hemisphere.

Yet not one of the individuals testifying before this committee mentioned the developing situation of dramatically increasing numbers of minors fleeing the Northern Triangle and crossing our border.

While the media is now highlighting this crisis, the fact is the administration knew about this months ago and, frankly, failed to put in place adequate resources to address the flow or develop a comprehensive response to the growing crisis.

Finally, earlier this year when Secretary Kerry was testifying before the full committee, I lamented the lack of action the Western Hemisphere was receiving from the administration.

I went on to ask him if he believed, with all the crises around the globe, if spending scarce resources on solar panels and abortion pills in Guatemala were the best use of taxpayer dollars.

To my utter surprise, the Secretary responded that climate change was the most significant crisis facing our country and the globe.

With all due respect, this situation of unaccompanied minors fleeing their homeland is an immediate crisis that demands an immediate response that focuses on development and jobs over pet environmental projects.

And to that end, when the money became available in the region from the closure of Ecuador and Bolivia missions those funds should have been retargeted toward addressing this UAC crisis, not spent on environmental intervention in Colombia, a middle-income nation.

Now is the time for USAID and State to make judicious use of taxpayers' hard earned money to help empower the people of these affected countries economically, to help them find ways to diversify their crops, to attract foreign investment, to encourage entrepreneurialism and economic freedom over a life of criminality and violence.

I am honored that the speaker appointed me to the congressional task force he constituted to look for solutions for this humanitarian crisis. I look forward to working with my colleagues and the administration to craft a swift, fair, appropriate and compassionate response to the crisis so we can get these children home with their families on a path to a more prosperous and secure region.

I am grateful to both Mr. Palmieri and Mr. Lopes for coming before this subcommittee today and I look forward to a constructive discussion on what we can do to mitigate the humanitarian crisis unfolding at our doorstep.

And I will now recognize the ranking member for his opening remarks.

Mr. SIRES. I am going to cede to the ranking member of the full committee, Congressman Engel.

Mr. ENGEL. Thank you. Thank you very much. I appreciate it, as I have to leave for another meeting. But I want to thank you, Mr. Chairman—Chairman Salmon—and Ranking Member Sires, for holding today's hearing on this important topic.

As the former chairman of the Western Hemisphere Subcommittee, I always feel at home coming back here to this subcommittee. This is a subcommittee where I have done some of my best work on the Foreign Affairs Committee as chairman and as ranking member as well, and as ranking member of the entire Foreign Affairs Committee, we always talk about the collaborative effort and the bipartisan effort that we always have on this committee.

I think it makes our committee stand up far behind any other committee in Congress in showing what Congress can do in working together, how much we can accomplish and I think of no better way than when it comes to foreign affairs that foreign policy, foreign relations should be done on a bipartisan basis because America is stronger when we have bipartisan support, and we obviously have very talented people on both sides of the aisle, and so it is a pleasure to see this being done again in a bipartisan fashion.

As a father, my heart goes out to all of the unaccompanied children making the dangerous trek from Central America to the United States. I know that some have responded to the large influx of children arriving in our country by calling for harsher enforcement of our immigration laws.

While we must continue to enforce our immigration statutes, cracking down on children is clearly not the answer. Last week, I sent a letter to the President which was signed by 61 of our House colleagues urging the administration to increase resources for programs that get at the root cause of unaccompanied children migrating here from Central America.

My letter calls for significant investments in State Department and USAID initiatives in El Salvador, Guatemala and Honduras that focus on youth gang prevention and economic development. It also urges funding for efforts designed to integrate returning children into their home countries.

This does not mean simply reprogramming existing funding, but instead means increasing the President's Fiscal Year 2015 request for Central America.

The administration justifiably increased the Department of Health and Human Services Office of Refugee Resettlement Fiscal Year 2015 request for its unaccompanied alien children program from $868 million to $2.28 billion.

Something similar can and should be done to provide funding that gets at the root causes of this migration pattern. I am pleased that Vice President Biden announced some added funding in Guatemala last Friday, and I was also pleased that the Senate Appropriations Committee increased funding for these programs.

Mr. Chairman, thank you again for holding today's hearing. As I have said at another forum previously, you have been a friend and partner of mine for many, many years and doing outstanding work as usual and as chairman of this subcommittee.

Mr. Sires, we have also worked together on so many different things, and it is really great seeing the two of you working together.

So I look forward to working with you and other members of this committee to increase foreign assistance to Central America to address the root causes of the current wave of child migration. Thank you.

Mr. SALMON. Thank you. Mr. Duncan.

Mr. DUNCAN. Thank you, Mr. Chairman, and thanks for the timeliness of this hearing. Some of the things I want to hear today, if you will take a look at that map right up there and you can't make out Guatemala, Honduras, El Salvador, but I know where they are.

I can see Mexico very, very clearly. That is a long way for these children to transit. It is hard for me to realize and comprehend that moms and dads would actually send children, and if you look at some of the pictures these kids are 3, 4, and 5 years old.

The moms and dads actually send them off that far on that kind of a journey unaccompanied. So I would like to find out if brothers and sisters are traveling with them, older teenage brother and sisters, parents, possibly transiting all the way through Mexico to get to the RGV.

I also want to hear today about this so-called aggressive public outreach campaign to counter false messages and accurately portray the dangers of the journey. Okay to accurately portray the danger of the journey, but I want to know what sort of counter false messages—I want to know what that means.

Are you saying don't come to America?—you will not get amnesty, you will not get citizenship—in fact, you will be deported back to your home country if you come—moms and dads, don't send those children to this country because they are going to be returned to you.

Chain migration is something that we should not allow. I want to hear what sort of message you are relaying into those countries because it has created a crisis situation on our border. We need a tourniquet down there. We need to stop the hemorrhaging of illegals flowing into this country. Not just the children. That is the topic of today—I realize that.

But we have a crisis situation on our border with folks entering our country that will eventually put a strain on our social services and our budget. We are $18 trillion in debt.

The President called for $1.8 billion humanitarian effort. Well, where does that money come from? It comes from taxpayers in South Carolina and Arizona to go to pay for unexpected folks that are coming into this country for a humanitarian effort, and so I want to talk a little bit about that today.

I appreciate what the State Department and what DHS is trying to do, and I appreciate this hearing, Mr. Chairman. I yield back.

Mr. SALMON. Thanks. Mr. Sires.

Mr. SIRES. Thank you, Mr. Chairman, for holding this hearing. I want to thank our witnesses for being here today. Over the past months we have been witness to an unprecedented number of child migrants coming to the U.S. from Central America, in particular the Northern Triangle countries of El Salvador, Guatemala and Honduras.

It is clear that the groundswell of unaccompanied child migrants arriving at the U.S.-Mexico border have resulted in a humanitarian crisis. This crisis will not be resolved overnight or with quick short fixes.

It will require dedicated shared responsibilities and regional response. For its part, the Congress must ensure that the U.S. authorities manage the processing of detained child migrants as humanely and transparently as possible while respecting their basic human rights and legal protection.

In turn, Northern Triangle governments must acknowledge common factors driving unaccompanied child migrants, specifically, the lack of economic opportunities and high levels of criminal violence in their home countries.

More importantly, it is incumbent upon the regions' governments to inform potential migrants and their families of the life-threatening dangers involved in the migratory journey and dispel any misgiving regarding current U.S. immigration policies, a status quo that remains unchanged.

Pronouncements that deny or implicitly ignore these factors exacerbate the unfolding crisis, do a disservice to the families that endure these stark realities every day and debilitate efforts in the Congress to provide further assistance that address the root causes of Central American child migration, let alone comprehensive immigration reform.

The Northern Triangle region in Central America is amongst the most violent in the world. According to the United Nations, Honduras is ranked first, El Salvador is ranked fourth, Guatemala is ranked fifth in terms of the highest murder rates in the country.

Since 2005, murders of men and boys increased 292 percent while the murders of women and girls increased 346 percent. In Honduras and El Salvador, in particular, child advocates reported increasing accounts of children being forcibly recruited to participate in gang activities.

Consequently, the number of Central American migrants comprising of a rising number of children from the Northern Triangle region have steadily increased.

In 2013, for the first time more than a third of the migrants whom the U.S. Border Patrol apprehended near the U.S.-Mexican border were other than Mexican—migrants comprised mainly of Honduras, El Salvador and Guatemala. Mexican child migrants accounted for 82 percent of the nearly 20,000 unaccompanied child apprehension in 2014 compared to 17 percent from the other three Northern Triangle countries.

Astonishingly, these proportions reversed within the first 8 months of 2014, with Mexican child migrants comprising only 25 percent of the roughly 47,000 unaccompanied child migrants apprehensions and child migrants from the northern region of the countries comprising an overwhelming 73 percent.

From Mexico, a country whose unaccompanied child migration numbers have declined but still serve as a primary thoroughfare for migrants from Central America, reports indicate that the migrants are increasingly citing widespread incident of extortion, kidnapping and other abuses committed by both criminal groups and Mexican federal, state and local police officials.

Mexico must work together with the Central American neighbors to address security concerns along the southern border, in addition to initiatives that strengthen institutions, sustaining the rule of law, and protect human rights.

This crisis has emerged within the backdrop of increasing foreign policy challenges, limited resources and a stalled effort to enact comprehensive immigration reform.

This crisis has not emerged halfway across the globe. It has unfolded at our own doorsteps, and underscores the need to pay appropriate attention to our own hemisphere.

Now more than ever, the U.S. should support the region in a concerted regional strategic strategy to increase economic opportunity, strengthen the rule of law, improve the integrity and effectiveness of police and security forces, and undermine the conditions that give way to gang and family-related violence.

These measures are futile, however, if not accompanied with a concerted effort to reintegrate these children back into their respective communities. Moreover, U.S. regional security aid programs like the Central American Regional Security Initiative must be dynamic enough to address ongoing citizen security concerns with the complementary programs designed to address underlying economic, social conditions that have communities vulnerable to criminal threats and ultimately result in immigration.

Vice President Biden visited the region's leaders and the administrations' announced plan to address the ongoing crisis are positive first steps.

However, with the Fiscal Year 2014 budget that has been reduced 20 percent to $130 million the U.S. must do more. This includes addressing the issues of millions of undocumented immigrants and their families.

I call upon the region's government to work with the United States and do their part to find solutions to this government—to this growing humanitarian crisis, provide a safe environment for the children and address the underpinning of what is compelling these young children to abandon their homeland to risk their lives to come to the U.S.

I look forward to hearing from our panelists and their assessment of how we can address this unfortunate crisis.

Mr. SALMON. Thank you. I understand Mr. Duffy does not have an opening statement. Is that correct? Mr. Castro, you are recognized.

Mr. CASTRO. First of all, thank you, Chairman and Ranking Member, for allowing me to join you today. Although I serve on the Foreign Affairs Committee, I am not on this subcommittee, so thank you.

The tragedy that is going on at our border is a direct result of the U.S. House of Representative's failure to pass comprehensive immigration reform. The fact is if we had passed either the Senate or the House bill, there were resources for both border security, international cooperation and it would have outlined a path for clear legal migration this country.

And yet as this has unfolded, everybody has been pointing fingers at each other—at the President, at the different parties—and the fact is that this body has failed the American people. We need to make sure, and the best thing that we can do is solve this situation, which is a humanitarian crisis.

I had a chance to visit Lackland Air Force Base, which is one of the emergency shelters that is housing the kids in San Antonio. I was told the story of a 6-year-old boy who traveled from I think it was Honduras with his 2-year-old sister, and during the journey they were separated and this kid was torn up because he thought his sister had died.

And they reunited them when they were both in custody and they were still held, and you all are right that there are rumors that the coyotes and the cartels are pitching to very desperate people. But the reason that those rumors are successful is because this Congress has failed to take real action on immigration reform.

So the very best thing that we can do to dispel those rumors and to create real change and fix this is to pass comprehensive reform, and I hope that we can do that this year. Thank you, Chair.

Mr. SALMON. Pursuant to Committee Rule 7, the members of the subcommittee will be permitted to submit written statements to be included in the official hearing record. Without objection, the hearing record will remain open for 7 days to allow statements, questions and extraneous materials for the record subject to the length limitation in the rules.

And now I am going to introduce the panel. First, we have Mr. Palmieri. He is the Deputy Secretary for Central America and Caribbean for the Bureau of Western Hemisphere Affairs and at the Department of State.

Prior to his current assignment, he served in the Dominican Republic, El Salvador, Honduras and as the senior desk officer for Venezuela. He has also led INL's Latin America and Caribbean Programs Office. Mr. Palmieri holds an M.S. in international strategic studies from the National War College and a B.A. in politics from Princeton University.

Mr. Lopes is the deputy assistant administrator for the Bureau of Latin America and Caribbean at USAID. Prior to joining USAID, he worked for the House Appropriations State Foreign Operations Subcommittee. He holds a B.M. from Berkeley College of Music and an M.P.P. from Harvard University's Kennedy School of Government.

You all understand the lighting system. When it goes amber you got a minute, and when it goes red it is time to stop. And so let us go ahead and begin.

Mr. Palmieri, we recognize you first.

STATEMENT OF MR. FRANCISCO PALMIERI, DEPUTY ASSISTANT SECRETARY FOR CENTRAL AMERICA AND THE CARIBBEAN, BUREAU OF WESTERN HEMISPHERE AFFAIRS, U.S. DEPARTMENT OF STATE

Mr. PALMIERI. Chairman Salmon, Ranking Member Sires, members of the subcommittee, I am very pleased to speak with you about the Department of State's role in addressing the migration of unaccompanied children to the United States, particularly from Central America.

I appreciate your attention to this important issue, and look forward to working with you. The administration is deeply concerned by the substantial increase over the past year in the number of children who are leaving their countries and attempting to migrate illegally to the United States.

We know that they are primarily arriving from El Salvador, Guatemala and Honduras. The number of children from those countries arriving at the southwest border has overwhelmed existing facilities.

The U.S. Government is working nonstop to arrange humane care for these children, consistent with U.S. legal requirements once they have arrived in the United States.

The Department of State in coordination with other agencies, with the Federal Emergency Management Agency in the lead, is working on a rapid government-wide response in the short-term while realigning our long-term efforts to address the systemic challenges in the region that drive migration.

Most importantly, at the senior levels of this administration, including the President, Vice President, Secretaries of State, Homeland Security and our Ambassadors in the region, we are engaging every day with our foreign government counterparts to help stem the flow of children leaving their countries.

We are doing this not just because it is part of enforcing our laws, but because it is the right thing to do to help these vulnerable children. Our first concern must be these children's safety.

Not only are these children exposed to life-threatening risks on the journey to the United States, but they are being misled about potential immigration benefits available in the United States.

For that reason, we are taking concrete steps to stop the spread of misinformation through criminal networks, which encourage these hazardous journeys.

To counter these messages, we and the Department of Homeland Security with Central American governments and Mexico, are developing new targeted public service announcements that will better reach the population centers that are the source of many of these vulnerable child migrants.

Our Embassies in all of these countries and in Mexico have launched aggressive public outreach campaigns to counter false messages and to accurately portray the dangers of the journey.

Our Ambassadors constantly engage with the media in these countries on this issue. Again, we are working hard to dispel the misguided notion that these children will not face deportation proceedings.

Our Mexican and Central American partners are cooperating fully in this messaging and deploying complementary information campaigns in their respective countries.

It is our goal that these information campaigns will better inform people in the region in order to prevent more children from making this incredibly dangerous journey.

The Vice President also announced last week in Guatemala that the administration will spend an additional $10 million in support of increased repatriation capacity and specialized training on procedures for receiving returned citizens.

In addition, the department continues to focus on a longer-term approach to address the systemic issue Central American countries face and are creating the push factors behind this phenomenon— lack of economic, educational and employment opportunities, weak institutions and high levels of violence and insecurity.

We are seeking to better balance our regional approach to prioritize and integrate prosperity, security and governance. We aim to address the need for job creation, attack insecurity and promote greater government accountability, all issues that are driving migrants, including these vulnerable children, to the United States.

Mexico also plays an important role in addressing this humanitarian situation, and we are working closely with the Government of Mexico on short and long-term solutions, given our shared responsibility for promoting security in both countries and in the region.

We are working to enhance our cooperation with Mexico to disrupt the organized criminal networks facilitating smuggling and strengthen their enforcement at Mexico's southern border with Guatemala. In addition, we are working with Mexico to increase enforcement along the dangerous La Bestia train route, which many of these most vulnerable migrants travel through Mexico.

From a foreign affairs perspective, we are using our existing resources to both manage the near-term surge in unaccompanied children, and to implement programs to address the long-term challenges that constitute the complex and systemic factors driving migration.

It is clear, however, that substantial transformative change in Central America requires greater efforts by all the actors involved, and we must work with Congress on this issue.

It is equally clear that a whole government approach and greater collaboration with international partners is required to control the extremely high cost of the domestic, humanitarian and law enforcement response.

Thank you, and I look forward to answering your questions.

[The prepared statement of Mr. Palmieri follows:]

**"Children Migrating from Central America:
Creating a Humanitarian Crisis"**

**Testimony before House Foreign Affairs Committee, Subcommittee
on the Western Hemisphere**

**Francisco Palmieri
Deputy Assistant Secretary
Bureau of Western Hemisphere Affairs
U.S. Department of State
Washington, DC**

Chairman Salmon, Ranking Member Sires, Members of the Committee, I am pleased to speak with you about the Department of State's role in addressing the migration of unaccompanied alien children to the United States, particularly from Central America. I appreciate your attention to this important issue and look forward to working with you.

The Administration is deeply concerned by the substantial increase over the past year in the number of unaccompanied children who are leaving their countries and attempting to immigrate illegally to the United States. We know that they are primarily arriving from El Salvador, Guatemala, and Honduras. The number of children from these countries arriving at the southwest border has overwhelmed existing facilities. The U.S. government is working non-stop to arrange humane care for these children, consistent with U.S. legal requirements, once they have arrived in the United States.

The Department of State, in coordination with other agencies, with the Federal Emergency Management Agency (FEMA) in the lead, is working on a rapid government-wide response in the short term, while realigning our broader, long-term efforts to address the systemic challenges in the region that drive migration. Most importantly, let me be clear: At the senior most levels of the Administration, to include the President, Vice President, Secretaries of State and Homeland Security, and the Department of State Counselor among others, we are engaging every day with our foreign government counterparts to help stem the flow of children leaving their countries. We are doing this not just because it is part of enforcing our laws, but because it is the right thing to do.

Not only are these children exposed to life-threatening risks on the journey to the United States, but there is the potential for them to be misled about potential immigration benefits available in the United States. Our first concern must be about these children's safety. For that reason we are taking concrete steps to stop the spread of misinformation through criminal networks, diaspora groups, and the media, which encourage these hazardous journeys. To counter these messages, we and the Department of Homeland Security (DHS) - with Central American governments and Mexico – are developing new targeted public service announcements that will better reach the population centers that are the source of many of these child migrants.

The State Department is funding additional public service announcements in El Salvador, Guatemala, and Honduras. Embassies in each of these countries – as well as in Mexico – have launched aggressive public outreach campaigns to counter false messages and accurately portray the dangers of the journey. Our Ambassadors and embassy officials constantly engage with the media in these countries. We are funding reporting tours and press briefings targeted at migrant communities. These reporting tours are bringing Central American journalists to U.S. Customs and Border Protection facilities on the border for discussions with Spanish-speaking DHS officials who can accurately explain U.S. immigration policy and emphasize the humane removal process for unaccompanied children. Again, we need to dispel the misguided notion that these children will not face deportation proceedings.

Our Mexican and Central American partners have been fully cooperative in this messaging endeavor and are working to develop and deploy complementary information campaigns in their respective countries. We hope these information campaigns help change the way of thinking that exists in the region in order to prevent more people from making this incredibly dangerous journey.

The Department will provide assistance to increase the capacity of the Central American governments to receive returned migrants. As the Vice President noted in Guatemala last week, the Administration will spend $9.6 million in support of increased capacity and to provide specialized training on procedures for receiving returned citizens.

Our short term objectives include increasing the repatriation capacity of Central American governments and improving media outreach on the dangers of the journey and to correct misperceptions about U.S. immigration law. In addition, the Department continues to focus on a longer-term approach to address the systemic issues Central American countries face and that are creating the push factors behind this phenomenon: lack of economic, educational, and employment opportunities, weak institutions, and high levels of violence and insecurity. In this respect, the Department of State is balancing our regional approach to prioritize and integrate prosperity, security, and governance. We aim to address the growth, insecurity, and accountability issues driving migrants, including unaccompanied children, to the United States.

The solution to the increase in illegal migration of unaccompanied children is not solely focused on Central America. Mexico plays an important role in addressing this humanitarian situation, and we are working closely with the Government of Mexico on short- and long-term solutions, given our shared responsibility for promoting security in both countries and in the region. During his call with the President last week, Mexican President Pena Nieto committed to working with us on this issue, including on the need to return children safely to their families, to build Central American capacity to receive returned children, and to address factors driving migration. The Vice President was pleased to have Mexican government Secretary Osorio Chong join the meeting in Guatemala last week. We are working to enhance our existing cooperation with Mexico to disrupt the organized criminal networks facilitating smuggling, strengthen enforcement at Mexico's southern border, and develop an information campaign that highlights both the dangers of the journey, and to dispel the misguided notion that these arriving migrants will not be subject to removal proceedings. While unaccompanied children from Central America are not eligible for expedited removal, they will be placed in removal proceedings and may be subject to deportation. Please note: unaccompanied children from Mexico may be repatriated immediately.

In addition, we are working closely with Mexico to increase enforcement along the dangerous "La Bestia" train route on which many of the most vulnerable migrants travel through Mexico.

From a foreign affairs perspective, we are using our existing resources to both manage the near-term surge in unaccompanied children and to implement programs to address the long-term challenges that constitute the complex and systematic factors driving migration. It is clear, however, that substantial, transformative change in Central America requires greater efforts by all the actors involved. It is equally clear that a whole of government approach and greater collaboration with international partners is required to avoid the extremely high costs of the domestic humanitarian and law enforcement response.

Thank you, and I look forward to answering your questions.

STATEMENT OF MR. MARK LOPES, DEPUTY ASSISTANT ADMIN-ISTRATOR, BUREAU FOR LATIN AMERICA AND THE CARIB-BEAN, U.S. AGENCY FOR INTERNATIONAL DEVELOPMENT

Mr. LOPES. Thank you, Chairman Salmon, Ranking Member Sires and members of the subcommittee. Thank you for the opportunity to discuss what the U.S. Agency for International Development is doing and can do to help curb the migration of unaccompanied children from Central America.

For several years, USAID programs in Guatemala, Honduras and El Salvador have worked to prevent violence and criminality and prevent youth from entering into gangs. USAID currently supports over 120 outreach centers across the region.

These centers are part of the portfolio of programs that make up USAID's contribution to the Central American Regional Security Initiative, which is a subset of programs that make up the overall $150 million USAID will invest in Guatemala, Honduras and El Salvador this year.

This broader investment includes programs in education, health, agriculture as well as the environment, and we see this integral approach to programming as the right way to carry out USAID's mission, which is to end extreme poverty and to promote resilient democratic societies while advancing our security and prosperity.

As Vice President Biden announced last Friday, USAID is launching a new 5-year $40 million program in Guatemala to improve citizen security to target particular communities and reduce the risk factors for young people to enter into violence.

In El Salvador, USAID recently announced a 5-year $25 million program that will open 77 new youth outreach centers, in addition to the 30 already in place there.

These centers, like those mentioned above, offer at-risk youth the chance to get help with their homework, get mentoring, computer training, or better yet, training on how to fix a computer so they can later get a job doing so.

USAID programs announced by Vice President Biden are part of a scaling up of prevention programs which reflect a recognition by our Government as well as by governments in the region that more financial and intellectual resources are required, to have a lasting impact on the root causes of violence and criminality.

In the last 5 years, this recognition is visible. Many governments in the region now have prevention-oriented strategies in place. This was not always the case.

USAID programs are designed to support those strategies and provide examples of that work so that the region's governments can expand and scale up in order to have a nationwide impact.

Recently, President Hernandez of Honduras publically committed to allocating 30 percent of the funds collected through their security tax to support programs in violence prevention.

Six hundred thousand dollars of the $1 million pledge from these Honduran resources has already been provided to expand the network of youth outreach centers across Honduras. This specific prevention-related programming by USAID is supported and integrated with our broader portfolio of work.

For example, in Guatemala, USAID will invest $25 million in a new program to improve access and quality of education for under-served populations, including indigenous children in 900 schools and vocational training for 2,000 out of school youth.

As part of our Feed the Future work, in Honduras USAID aims to lift 50,000 families out of extreme poverty, reduce stunting of children under 5 by 20 percent and improve more than 280 kilometers of rural roads, providing market access to thousands and thus improving economic prosperity.

In addition, the private sector has a role and USAID is aggressively pursuing partnerships with the private sector both here in the United States as well as in the region, as civil society organizations bring more resources and more creativity to bear.

In the last several years, USAID has leveraged approximately $40 million for partnerships with companies, local organizations and local governments in the region. For example, in El Salvador we are partnering with Microsoft to provide computer software and training to outreach centers to reach 25,000 youth in 13 high-risk municipalities.

Our prevention efforts are designed both to have an immediate and measurable impact, but more importantly, to prove concepts and demonstrate that such investments can provide dividends beyond their cost.

Preliminary findings from a 3-year impact evaluation provides statistically significant evidence that crime rates are lower and public perception of security is higher in the areas in which we work. This is good news, but the efforts need to be scaled up to see an impact on national level statistics.

Mr. Chairman, USAID is well positioned when done in partnership with governments and the private sector in the region, and when successful programs are taken to scale to help improve economic and social well being in the region.

By working together to keep children in school, train out of school youth for jobs and connect small farmers to markets as well as creating entry points for historically marginalized groups, the region can become more secure and prosperous for the long-term.

This has been, and will continue to be, a principal focus for USAID and these efforts will continue to benefit citizens throughout the Americas. Thank you, and I look forward to answering any questions you may have.

[The prepared statement of Mr. Lopes follows:]

Testimony of Mark Lopes
Deputy Assistant Administrator for Latin America and the Caribbean
U.S. Agency for International Development
House Committee on Foreign Affairs
June 25, 2014, 2:00 p.m.
"Children Migrating from Central America: Creating a Humanitarian Crisis"

Chairman Salmon, Ranking Member Sires, Members of the Subcommittee, thank you for the opportunity to discuss what the U.S. Government, in particular the U.S. Agency for International Development (USAID), is doing and can do in the future to help curb the influx of unaccompanied children from Central America arriving to the U.S. border. As stated in our new mission statement, USAID partners to end extreme poverty and to promote resilient, democratic societies while advancing our security and prosperity. In line with this mission USAID's programs remain committed to addressing the root causes of insecurity and lack of opportunity in the region, and I am happy to discuss these programs with you today.

Pending final Congressional approval, USAID expects to implement up to $150 million in this fiscal year to address the root causes of crime and violence in Honduras, Guatemala, and El Salvador. Of this amount, approximately $50 million is specifically designated programs for at-risk youth. Through the Central America Regional Security Initiative (CARSI), we are investing in opportunities for youth and their communities and strengthening the institutions charged with administering justice to keep people safe. Our services for at-risk youth, job training, community policing, safe urban spaces and juvenile justice programs complement the youth-focused cultural and educational programs as well as the law enforcement and interdiction activities led by our inter-agency partners.

As Vice President Biden announced last Friday, USAID is launching a new five-year $40-million program this summer in Guatemala to improve citizen security. This program will target hotspot communities for migration, poverty, and extreme violence to reduce the risk factors for youth involvement in gangs and help mitigate the push factors for potential migration to the United States.

In El Salvador, USAID is carrying out a new five-year $25-million crime and violence prevention program that will open an additional 77 youth outreach centers in addition to the 30 already in existence. These centers offer services to at-risk youth who are susceptible to gang recruitment.

In Honduras, USAID funds 40 youth outreach centers in hotspot communities like San Pedro Sula with more to come over the next year. These programs are part of a scaling-up of prevention programs, which reflects recognition by our government as well as governments in the region that more financial and intellectual resources are required to have a lasting impact on the root causes of violence and criminality. Many governments in the region now have prevention-oriented strategies in place. USAID's programs are designed to support those strategies and provide examples of programs that are successful, so that the region's governments can expand and scale-up programs to have a country-wide impact.

Recently, President Hernandez of Honduras publicly committed to allocating 30 percent of the funds collected through Honduras' new Security Tax to support prevention programs. President Hernandez has already provided $600,000 of a $1 million pledge to expand the network of youth outreach centers across the country.

USAID's CARSI programming complements our traditional development programs aimed at creating jobs in rural and urban communities, improving early grade literacy, improving food security, and investing in small and medium sized businesses.

In Guatemala, for example, USAID will invest nearly $25 million in a new program to improve access to and quality of education for under-served populations, including rural indigenous girls and boys in 900 rural schools, and educational and vocational training opportunities for 2,000 out-of-school youth.

As part of our Feed the Future work, in Honduras USAID has contributed $24.5 million to the new Dry Corridor Initiative, a multi-donor and Government of Honduras initiative to promote sustainable agricultural development of the country's southwest border area. Through this work we aim to lift 50,000 families out of extreme poverty, reduce stunting of children under 5 by 20 percent, and improve more than 280 kilometers of rural roads, providing market access to thousands and improving economic prosperity.

USAID also continues to successfully utilize partnerships, as part of our new model of development, with companies and other private sector leaders to promote youth engagement and prevent youth from joining gangs. In the last several years, USAID has leveraged approximately $40 million for partnerships with companies, local organizations and governments working with at-risk youth in the Northern triangle countries of Central America.

For instance, in El Salvador USAID is partnering with Microsoft to provide computer software and training for youth at outreach centers in 13 high-risk municipalities. Through this partnership, about 25,000 youth will have access to training. In addition, Microsoft will establish over a dozen technology academies that will provide youth participants with a path to certification in specialized computer training and competitive labor skills.

To ramp up these efforts, the Vice President recently announced an open call to the private sector – companies, private foundations and NGOs – to join forces with USAID to co-fund innovative partnerships, through USAID's Global Development Lab, which will be designed to increase educational and economic opportunities for at-risk youth in Guatemala, Honduras, and El Salvador.

Our prevention efforts are designed both to have an immediate and measurable impact, but more importantly to prove concepts and demonstrate that such investments can pay dividends beyond their cost. USAID has tested a range of approaches that were used both in the United States and around region. Now that preliminary findings from a three-year impact evaluation provide statistically significant evidence that crime rates are lower and public perception of security higher in the areas in which we work, we are working to scale up the most promising approaches. More importantly, we are looking to the governments in the region to adopt the most successful of these efforts and incorporate the lessons learned or the programs themselves into their efforts.

USAID has already begun to expand our efforts to create safe spaces for youth to retreat from violence and receive valuable job training. Today, we have a network of 120 outreach centers in violent communities across the region. In Honduras alone, tens of thousands of youth vulnerable to the lure of crime received assistance through 40 such centers operating in four of the country's most violent cities.

Mr. Chairman, USAID is well positioned to help address the long-term drivers of insecurity and social, economic and environmental challenges in the region. However, a sustained and long-term impact at the national level is only possible when our successes are incorporated into the work of the governments in the region.

Limited donor resources alone are insufficient to incent the kind of transformative change needed to create widespread opportunity over the long run. The affected governments in the region, along with multilateral development banks and others in the donor community, must also prioritize investments – beyond crime prevention and law enforcement -- that address the root causes of the migration phenomena we are seeing today.

Only by working together to keep children in school, train out-of-school youth for higher education or jobs, connect small farmers to local and regional markets, and create entry points for historically marginalized groups will the region become more secure and prosperous for the long term. This has been and will continue to be a principal focus for USAID, and will continue to benefit citizens throughout the Americas.

Thank you and I look forward to answering any questions you may have.

Mr. SALMON. Thank you. I thank the witnesses for their testi-monies. I will yield myself 5 minutes, and then will proceed with the ranking member and thank the witnesses.

Mr. Lopes, thank you for your testimony and for outlining the various ways USAID has been working to improve the situation in Central America.

Unfortunately, I have seen many of your colleagues come up to the Hill to deliver notifications on one program or another, but al-ways lacking in specificity. The American people are, as you know, exceedingly generous in providing aid to countries in need to im-prove the lives of their citizens.

Indeed, USAID efforts in Mexico and Central America can have a direct impact on our own security and lives, as this current crisis reflects. Enforced immigration laws combined with economic oppor-tunity and security in Central America would have kept young chil-dren in their countries with their families.

What I am saying is that I am supportive of USAID's efforts to help empower the nations of Central America as long as the money that we are spending is effective and efficient.

I would like to see a comprehensive list country by country, project by project, including costs, implementing partner details and how specifically the said project directly helps the crisis level in security and lack of economic opportunity we are seeing in some Central American countries today, namely, the three that we have talked about. Can you provide me with those details?

This level of specificity would go a long way in helping us to evaluate the effectiveness of our efforts there while being truly ac-countable to the taxpayer, and I think you would agree that we owe the taxpayer at least that.

Mr. LOPES. Absolutely, Congressman. Yes, we can provide that information and certainly willing to work with your office and happy to come up and make sure that you have——

Mr. SALMON. That would be great.

Mr. LOPES [continuing]. A comprehensive set.

Mr. SALMON. And I will share it with the committee when I get that.

Mr. LOPES. Absolutely, and I also referenced in my opening state-ment one of the efforts that we have done to do a scientific analysis of the impact of our programs. This was an effort with Vanderbilt University to look at control groups and treatment groups——

Mr. SALMON. Right.

Mr. LOPES [continuing]. In communities where we had an im-pact, and we have seen statistically significant progress in the areas in which we work.

Mr. SALMON. Can we get those reports too? That would be great.

Mr. LOPES. I'd be happy to share that with you.

Mr. SALMON. Thank you very much. And then I am going to ask one last question, and then I am going to ask Mr. Duncan to take over the chair for just a few minutes. I have got another thing I have got to attend to.

But with both of you—with the USAID mission in Ecuador clos-ing and our mission in the diplomatic environment in Bolivia it continues to present difficulties for our officers since the closing of USAID and the expulsion of our Ambassador there.

Have State and USAID been looking for ways to redirect funding otherwise intended for Ecuador and Bolivia potentially going to address this crisis and working with Central America? I understand that some of the Ecuador USAID money is now going to environmental projects in Colombia and Jamaica.

While I don't intend to denigrate the potential long-term benefits of sensitizing our neighbors to environmental stewardship, I would submit to you that this is maybe a far more immediate crisis and maybe we should try to direct some of that money to this crisis as well.

Is that something that could be within the realm of possibility?

Mr. LOPES. I can speak to that, Congressman. Happy to outline. With respect to the Ecuador money, that money was already designated to go to environment programs, particularly in the Andean Amazon. So we did not have the flexibility to divert those resources toward crime prevention programs in Central America.

But that is the kind of flexibility that certainly we benefit from and our ability to have fully funded accounts as well as the flexibility to move those resources accordingly certainly helps us pivot quickly and direct resources toward where they are needed.

Over the last several years, we have seen a shift in budgetary priorities from South America to Central America. In these budget times, a flatline is the new increase and that is where we have preserved resources for Central America, particularly focused on Guatemala, El Salvador and Honduras, to make sure that those countries, and particularly the efforts on crime prevention, were the overarching focus of USAID's work there combined with a series of other economic prosperity programs that we see as a part of the entire package toward having real jobs and real opportunities over the long run.

So certainly the flexibility to provide those resources is useful, and we are happy to work with you to figure out what kind of things can be freed up looking——

Mr. SALMON. Well, if there is anything that we can do to maximize that flexibility so that we can get the money to where we have actually got the problems—the most immediate problems— then I think we are all interested in a bipartisan way to get that done.

I am going to yield back and ask the gentleman. He is next.

Mr. DUNCAN. The Chair recognizes Mr. Sires from New Jersey.

Mr. SIRES. Thank you very much. This past week the Hispanic Caucus called a number of members to meet with some of the Ambassadors of these countries because of this crisis, and it was very disappointing to me that we had 13 members and only one——

Mr. DUNCAN. If we could start the clock back at 5 minutes just due to the interruption in the back.

Mr. SIRES. Thank you. It was very disappointing to me that only one Ambassador showed up, and I let him know that we were all very disappointed because we all have our schedule.

So my question to you basically is how serious or seriously are these countries taking the effort to deal with this humanitarian crisis?

Because that to me was a sign that all they are looking for is they have a pressure cooker in their own country and this is one way of releasing some of that pressure and, you know, I am here to work—I have been here 8 years.

I try to work as much as I can on a bipartisan basis to try to deal with some of these problems in the Western Hemisphere, especially these countries.

But to have a situation like this and not have the decency to show up where 13 members who are their best supporters just makes it more difficult for us to assist them and more difficult for us to come up with some sort of immigration reform.

So I am asking you in your dealings with some of these Ambassadors, some of these countries, give me a perception—your perception of how seriously do they take this, or they are saying just send them to America and the pressure is off us.

Mr. PALMIERI. Thank you, Mr. Sires. The three Ambassadors from El Salvador, Honduras and Guatemala are all working very hard and have had extensive engagements with the administration.

But more importantly than their engagements with us is the real work that they are doing to get additional consular personnel from their Embassies to the border region to facilitate the processing of these arrivals and ensuring the documents that they need to be able to identify these children——

Mr. SIRES. You know, that is all well and good. But I want to know what they are doing in their country to stymie this exodus, because this is a humanitarian crisis. You have kids as young as 5, young as 6.

Just give me your opinion on what they are doing—what are they actually doing in their own country. And I must say that I am very proud of the way this country has handled those children because we have provided to them on a humanitarian basis. We have taken care of them. But I want to know what is going on in their own country.

Mr. PALMIERI. In Guatemala, El Salvador and Honduras, senior leaders across the spectrum—the Presidents, the foreign ministries—have been very active in echoing the messages about the dangers of the journey, about the real vulnerability these children suffer as they make that journey and are taking steps in Honduras.

The President of Honduras has redirected their border enforcement units to focus on alien smuggling networks, and to try to make a more effective interdiction of children leaving the San Pedro Sula area.

He is dedicated and called together an inter-institutional committee to address children's issues in the country with a direct focus on trying to stop the children from leaving.

They all realize—all three countries' leaders realize how vulnerable and exploited these children can be on this dangerous journey. In Guatemala, President Perez Molina has issued statements as well, and in one province along the migration route through Guatemala there was a recent arrest of a police official who apparently was facilitating some of this type of smuggling.

In El Salvador, likewise, the Foreign Minister and the President have been equally vocal about the real threat that their children are suffering when they make this journey and complementing the messages that we are saying, that there are no immigration benefits when these children arrive at the border.

Mr. SIRES. Do they recognize how difficult they make it on this Congress to come up with a comprehensive immigration reform when these things happen? Mr. Lopes, do you know?

Mr. PALMIERI. I think all three countries understand that the arrival of these unaccompanied children at the border will complicate and is complicating efforts to promote comprehensive immigration reform.

Mr. LOPES. I think just a couple of examples from our side, one that I mentioned in my testimony in terms of the 30 percent—I am sorry, the $600,000 of the $1 million pledge of Honduran resources, that is part of a commitment to use funds from a new security tax—30 percent of those for prevention activities.

I am persuaded when governments put forward real money and they put forward that money toward backing prevention programs. So that is a positive. In addition, there is an asset seizure law where the proceeds from those seized assets end up going back to municipalities where those assets receive to help work on prevention programs in those municipalities, so that there is incentive for those municipalities to seize those assets, to then see those resources coming back around to help on the prevention side.

Those are the kinds of partnerships beyond strategies which all free countries have which we see as new. The days of recognizing that prevention is an important piece of this are relatively new.

Ten years ago, we wouldn't have been talking about the governments in the region being so acutely oriented toward the importance of social programs of economic opportunity, but rather focused more on law enforcement and efforts to punish people for a deviation from laws.

Mr. SIRES. My time is up. Thank you, Mr. Chairman.

Mr. DUNCAN. I thank the gentleman. I recognize myself for 5 minutes.

This is a screen shot. This is one of the children. We are not talking about teenagers here. We are talking about very, very young— don't you love an iPad? You touch it in the wrong place and it goes away.

It is a little girl. I would say she was probably, what, Sean, you got small children. Three? Three years old? She's coloring. All right.

So what we are talking about if you look at that map, that area right there where that dot is dancing is the Guatemala-Honduras area, the Mexican border. Brownsville, Texas is right here, the Rio Grande Valley.

From the capital city of Honduras to Brownsville is well over 1,000 miles. Sean, could your 3-year-old travel 1,000 miles without you, without your adult children, your older children accompanying them? I don't think so.

The question I have is this. Historically, this border right here between Guatemala and Mexico has been one of the hardest places in the world to get through. What is Mexico doing to help us in this issue?

What has changed within the country of Mexico that it has allowed 60,0000 children to transit that area? Whether they are Honduran or Guatemalan or El Salvadorean, they crossed that border and they came through Mexico to get to the United States.

They didn't get on an airplane. They walked or they rode a train or in a car or something and we are talking about, what, 3-year-olds? So what has changed within Mexico and that border situation? Mr. Palmieri.

Mr. PALMIERI. Thank you, Mr. Duncan. Mexico is working very hard with us to address these conditions, particularly on their southern border.

We are looking at redirecting some of our foreign assistance through the Merida initiative to help strengthen Mexican interdiction efforts along their southern border. They have a southern border strategy that they have been executing. I think they are working very hard with us to try to have an impact on this flow and——

Mr. DUNCAN. But what has changed? Because historically it is a tough border to cross. What has changed? What has changed in Mexico?

Mr. PALMIERI. I think that the alien smuggling networks have begun to prey on families' willingness to send these children, and they are using some of their other established smuggling routes to move these children through the region.

But the Mexican Government's commitment to work with us on this has been reaffirmed and they are working closely with us because they understand the true human costs to these children and the need for better border enforcement and to work with the three countries in Central America to help stem this flow.

Mr. DUNCAN. Let me shift gears for just a minute, because we have talked a lot about funding today. The administration has promised a series of new foreign assistance programs for Central American countries.

However, according to a 2013—January of 2013 GAO report less than 28 percent of the funds appropriated from the year 2008 through the Fiscal Year 2011 have been disbursed. Why is this? And hold that question.

Why is it necessary to make additional foreign assistance commitments when you have not even used all the money that Congress have given you? And Mr. Lopes, you are fine to answer that—one of you.

Mr. LOPES. Sure. Thank you. I think what was referenced in the GAO report is what we call pipeline, which is a build-up of resources that have yet to go out the door. My understanding is that pipeline is significantly diminished.

We are happy to provide you an updated set of information with respect to those figures but also to say that, you know, the efforts that we have undertaken as USAID to ramp up our spending in these prevention efforts there is an absorptive capacity limit that is not something we can go from zero to $100 million from one day to the next.

It takes some time to build that up. We have been in that process for several years, and I think we are well positioned.

You saw some recent announcement by President—I am sorry, Vice President Biden with respect to new programs in the region—large-scale programs. We have now up to 120 outreach centers. So we are to a point where we are able to spend and move resources much more quickly. That is positive.

In addition, we are also partnering with private sector and leveraging other funds from the private sector to get resources there. Resources there are certainly not the only piece of it.

We need the kind of partnership that Mr. Palmieri was talking about from the governments in the region, from other actors that care about the outcome. The private sector is one that we have really aggressively reached out to because they care about security as well. It is a business issue for them. It is a bottom line issue.

It affects their bottom line when people can't get to work on the buses. And so we have, through a series of partnerships and creative efforts, to get cameras on buses in San Pedro Sula, Honduras to get a police force that monitors those cameras.

There are 54 cameras spread throughout the buses because they saw that buses is where the crimes are taking place and so what about a creative solution to work with the private sector there.

Another effort is to get the private sector to donate street lamps. Those street lamps are then upgraded by the national electric utility, and the businesses get the benefit of those lights and everyone benefits from security.

So it takes some time. We think we are there and we are getting to a point where we can spend a lot more and a lot faster.

Mr. DUNCAN. I appreciate your comment. You kept going back to private sector, and we are talking about public sector dollars in programs to foreign countries, and I understand the public-private partnership and how USAID works. But let me just say this and then end the time here.

I understand the humanitarian side of this. I am very sympathetic to the children that are there. I want what is best for them.

But I also am very concerned about the national sovereignty of this nation and our porous southern border and also elements that may be coming along with the children that are transiting into our country and what they are coming for. So I think you are going to need to be able to answer that question.

If you are going to ask me to provide a vote for more dollars for foreign aid to Central America, you are going to have to able to provide a little bit more explanation of why this money hasn't been spent or an explanation of how it has been if not allocated dedicated—that is, future expenditures and how it is going to be spent.

Whether that is a graph or whether that is information to this committee, I think we deserve that if we are going to actually cast a vote to provide you more dollars.

And with that, I will yield to the gentleman, Mr. Meeks.

Mr. MEEKS. Thank you. You know, just seems to me when I think about the creation of our country it was from individuals that were fleeing bad situations to a better situation.

It is almost just human nature if you see something that is better you try to get to what is better and you want your child to have a better life than you have had. And so it is difficult, and based upon what I know specifically about this problem I would like to emphasize a few things real quickly, then ask a couple of questions because I think that this should be a wake-up call, number one—a wake up call that would cause us to refocus our attention on the Western Hemisphere—our region of the world.

Current migration patterns demonstrate if we don't pay attention to what is happening just beyond our borders it will be to our own children. While the headlines of the day may draw attention to far-away places like Iraq and Iran and Ukraine and, make no mistake, these are important issues that also demand our attention, but we must not lose sight of what is happening closer to home.

The reality is truly terrifying when you think about homicide rates and when you think about the fact that maybe a third of everybody in either whether it is Guatemalans, Hondurans or Salvadorans report being victims of a crime within the last year, the statistics go on. They are just staggering.

Secondly, this is a serious humanitarian crisis which demands the attention of both our domestic and foreign policy experts, and we must study the underlying social and economic factors present in these countries.

Lastly, we must also understand the inherent interconnectedness of the Americas and indeed of the global village at large. Gone are the days when we could analyze a country's domestic problems in a vacuum and as a result of the globalization problems like this one we must have a bipartisan, which I think we are trying to do in this committee, and multilateral strategies to rid Latin America and the Caribbean of the violence and gangs which are leaving our children with no option but to flee their homes in pursuit of a brighter future.

That being said, I have been a long champion of trade capacity building. It was a significant part of the CAFTA negotiations in 2003 and 2004. In fact, it was the determining factor on why I was one of the few Democrats that voted for CAFTA because of the money that was put into trade capacity building.

So that was part of it. It was millions of dollars we appropriated for this and USAID received a large percentage of these funds as well as a large percentage of the responsibility for ensuring that they were used wisely.

So my question is have you been able to provide—and this is for either Mr. Lopes or Mr. Palmieri—an update or can you provide an update on the status of these funds and how have they been spent?

Mr. LOPES. Certainly. Thank you, Congressman. I would like to give you a comprehensive written response to that to make sure that we cover all the funds.

My understanding of those resources during the time of the CAFTA program is that there was a period of years through which there was a set amount that was dedicated toward particular training activities to dedicate resources to compensate for what was seen as shortcomings in their ability to carry out and to implement the Central American Free Trade Agreement.

A lot of those efforts have run their course although, and so some of those programs I think have closed and resources have been dedicated toward new areas or ongoing priorities.

I think it is certainly worth a look to ensure that the purposes for which those funds were dedicated have stuck, and that the capacities that we have put in there are still strong and that those trade agreements are still working.

I am not sure to what extent there is a scope for USAID to engage in that or resources to follow up, but certainly I think a conversation around ensuring that any economic capacity building resources are being used as effectively as possible, and our office is happy to engage with yours on that.

Mr. PALMIERI. In addition, I think CAFTA–DR has had a measurable positive impact. The central economy—the Central American economies on average have doubled their GDP over the last 10 years.

Exports to the United States through CAFTA are up 66 percent. While CAFTA is not the only component of our program in the region, it is making a significant impact in contributions in some of the root conditions.

Mr. MEEKS. But here is the—here is the issue, and we have some of it here. You know, we talk about GDP and that is good.

But sometimes that does not translate down to the common person who is trying to get a job and want to better themselves and improve their families. So the GDP sounds good for maybe 1 or 2 percent at the top but what about everyone else?

And that was part of what—the capacity building so that the jobs that would be created—it was about creating jobs here in America but also importantly about creating jobs there because guess what, folks? If we create jobs there they won't come here. You know, they come here for opportunity.

So that is what is important to get done. So I would like to see a comprehensive report to look at the jobs that we could have created there so that individuals have an opportunity and then talk about the security network that surrounds that, because if that happens then we don't have to worry about, you know, people crossing our borders all the time.

Mr. PALMIERI. Yes, sir.

Mr. DUNCAN. I thank the gentleman for his comments and the Chair recognizes Mr. Duffy from Wisconsin.

Mr. DUFFY. Thank you, Mr. Chairman. In my short time here in Congress—3½ years—I don't think I have seen an issue that has made me more angry than seeing 4-year-olds and 6-year-olds and 8-year-olds by themselves with smugglers or coyotes coming to the American border.

I have kids those age—4, 6, 8, 10, 12, 14—a lot of them. And I could tell you what, to think that they could be traveling on their own to the American border is absolutely outrageous and that our Government has played a part in this push—in the pull of the push and pull is absolutely outrageous and it is unacceptable.

Mr. Palmieri, in your comments about—oh, let me—I won't go there. Do you have a report for us about what kind of horrors these children experience during their 100-plus—hundreds of miles journey here? Rape, abuse, murder? What information do you have on what they experience on their route to America?

Mr. PALMIERI. The journey is incredibly dangerous and——

Mr. DUFFY. I know that. What specifics do you have?

Mr. PALMIERI. And we know that individuals and children in particular who undertake that journey suffer different forms of violence. They could be sexually——

Mr. DUFFY. Have you done studies?

Mr. PALMIERI [continuing]. There are reports of sexual assault. There are reports of mass killings in the past. There are reports of being kidnapped, and then extorted for additional funds as they are crossing along the journey.

There are reports of children who have been maimed trying to board trains that are moving to the north. The dangers are significant. They are very well documented, and we can get you a full report on that.

Mr. DUFFY. I would welcome that. Are you a parent?

Mr. PALMIERI. I am a parent, and I also——

Mr. DUFFY. Okay. I just want to ask you a question. So do you think that you need your government to tell you that—I don't know how old your children are, but if you have a 4-year-old do you need the government to say, listen, you are going to send your child, your 4-year-old or your 6-year-old, on a multiple 100-mile journey?

It is dangerous. You don't know the coyote. You don't know the smuggler. News flash to all of you who want to spend money to go, this is a dangerous trip for my child. I would say that is pointless.

It muddies the message, and you told us that is part of the messaging that you are doing in these countries. I think it makes more sense to say the American border is closed. This trip will be for naught. If you get there, I am sorry. We are compassionate.

The President has talked about our DREAMers. But if you come you are going to be sent back. Don't make the trip. But that you are telling parents that this is dangerous, parents aren't stupid. I mean, this is insulting that you tell a parent that it is a dangerous trip.

Mr. PALMIERI. The messages combine both messages, Mr. Duffy. Not only are we explaining the dangers of the journey and making it very real for these parents to consider, but we are also making clear that there are no immigration benefits in the United States when you arrive.

Mr. DUFFY. Are you telling them that the border——

Mr. PALMIERI. That there will be no——

Mr. DUFFY. So to that point are——

Mr. PALMIERI [continuing]. Benefit under the deferred action on childhood arrivals, that there will be no benefit under comprehensive immigration reform.

Mr. DUFFY. And to back up that point, have you been sending any of these children back home?

Mr. PALMIERI. There have been very few——

Mr. DUFFY. That is right. There has been very few. So isn't——

Mr. PALMIERI [continuing]. Deportations of the unaccompanied children because we have to first attend to their humanitarian needs——

Mr. DUFFY. So wouldn't the message——

Mr. PALMIERI [continuing]. And connect them to a guardian or a relative who can receive them.

Mr. DUFFY. So the message really is you send them and they don't get deported. They haven't been deported. They get to stay.

You can say all you want but the messaging has been if you send your children to the American—the U.S. border they will be allowed in and they won't be sent back to the country of origin, and I think that is the wrong message. And you would agree that this is a humanitarian crisis that involves children, yes?

Mr. PALMIERI. It is an acute humanitarian situation these children are suffering.

Mr. DUFFY. What is the pull that has brought these kids to the United States?

Mr. PALMIERI. The factors we see, and it is a very complex issue as you have just outlined, is there are factors both in their home country related to——

Mr. DUFFY. That is the push. I'm talking about what is the pull. What is the pull bringing them up here?

Mr. PALMIERI. And they have family members, obviously, in the United States that they are trying to reunite.

Mr. DUFFY. Do you think it has anything to do with the President's comments about immigration—the President's policies on our border?

Mr. PALMIERI. I think the administration's message has been very clear since this situation has expanded, that there are no immigration benefits for these children who are arriving; that they will be given notices to appear for deportation proceedings and that the journey will be futile.

Mr. DUFFY. This is a humanitarian crisis that involves children. I think it is of the utmost seriousness. What comments publicly has the President made to say listen, our borders aren't open and if you send your children they will be deported back to their country of origin? What public comments has he made to that effect?

Mr. PALMIERI. The messages we are sending out are really loud and clear.

Mr. DUFFY. That is not my question for you. No, no, no, no. My question is what has—this is serious stuff. It involves children. What has the President said publicly about sending these children home? He hasn't said anything, has he?

Mr. PALMIERI. I will gather the President's statements and deliver them.

Mr. DUFFY. He has—he has made public statements to this effect? I haven't seen them. I haven't heard them. You have?

Mr. PALMIERI. In the announcement about the humanitarian situation, the President emphasized that we had a humanitarian need.

Mr. DUFFY. Did he say that our borders were closed? I mean, it is a humanitarian crisis but he is not saying listen, of course, it is a humanitarian crisis but listen everybody, our borders are closed. If you come we are going to send you back home.

That would go a long way to sending the message to these specific three countries that if you send your kids it is dangerous, and they are not going to get the benefit that you talked about in your testimony.

If the President says that, that goes a long way and I think save the little kids' lives. I used to prosecute child sexual assault cases.

They are the most horrific cases that you will ever handle as a prosecutor, and to think that these kids will go through these horrors and the President won't stand up and say listen, there is no benefit—please don't send your children, and he says it publicly and strongly. I think that is the wrong message from this administration. I yield back.

Mr. SALMON. Thank you. Mr. Smith.

Mr. SMITH. Thank you very much and I want to thank my friend, Mr. Duffy, for raising the issue. This is serious stuff and we all get it.

Like my colleagues, I am extremely concerned about the welfare and well being of these children. Back in the early 1980s, I wrote the Child Survival Fund, put it at $50 million and went to El Salvador when there was a day of tranquility when the FMLN and Napoleon Duarte had a cease fire simply to vaccinate children against polio, diphtheria, pertussis.

So members of this panel and Mr. Duffy, as having prosecuted some of these horrific cases, we are in solidarity with these children. We are deeply concerned about it.

So I would like to ask a few very specific questions because they are vulnerable to sickness. They are vulnerable to abuse and even death. I have worked on neglected tropical diseases for the entirety of my 34 years as a Member of Congress.

We have a bill pending that deals with that. Last year I had a hearing on NTDs by one of the greatest experts in the world, Peter Hotez, ''Forgotten People, Forgotten Diseases.'' He points out that in this very incisive book as you know, I'm sure, to my friend from USAID, the places where these kids are coming from are endemic with hookworm, roundworm, whipworm and many, many other parasitic infections.

This long journey, the strain on their young and very fragile beings, certainly can exacerbate those problems. So first question, are U.S. medical personnel screening for NTDs?

Are they asking the right questions, doing the right kind of analysis to determine whether or not a child is carrying worms which certainly makes him or her vulnerable to other opportunistic infections?

Secondly, on human trafficking, I am the author of the Trafficking Victims Protection Act of 2000. It is the bill, the landmark bill on combating trafficking, yet in my own district in Lakewood we had a situation where a Mexican trafficker had a number of Mexican women and young girls.

That was busted. They are being prosecuted. We have Honduran gangs in Trenton. They are doing the same thing with mostly Honduran young girls and we know it is everywhere.

Gangs have not replaced but have been added to the issue or the exploiters and we know that these gangs, including some of these gangs coming out of Central America, are exploiting young girls and young women.

So my question would be about trafficking. What is being done to mitigate the possibility and, I would say, high probability of these girls and young women being forced into prostitution and to other kind of servitude?

There was a report that just came out, and I would commend it to your reading that something on the order of 90 percent—88 percent was the number they give—of trafficked women at some point have contact with a health care provider.

About 60 percent are emergency rooms, and yet, from the interviews of well over 100 trafficked women it was discovered with shock and dismay that they never asked, even though there was bruising, there were other kinds of indicators of abuse, whether or not that woman was in trouble and needed to be rescued.

My hope is that our health officials and others will be looking for the telltale signs, many of which are subtle but looking for them nevertheless to ask the right questions—are you being trafficked, are you being exploited? Because that is a huge problem.

You know, we see it with tsunamis and with hurricanes. We were very concerned when the hurricane or typhoon hit the Philippines, and I went to the Philippines. Every question I asked was about what is being done to ensure the exploited are not and USAID did a wonderful job, frankly, during that typhoon period to ensure that that didn't happen.

I know I will run out of time, but HHS is vetting—when people are handed over and children are handed over to relations that might be family how are they vetting to ensure that who that child is passed over to is not an abuser, a trafficker or someone purporting to be a family member?

Are they overwhelmed to the point where they are contracting that out? Because that would be a serious problem. I mean, how well—you know, we don't want to find 6 months from now that kids have been passed over to trafficking rings, and it can happen.

It can happen very easily when you have an overflow of crisis like this. So if you could touch on that as well. And finally, the administration is pushing fast track of the Trans-Pacific Partnership and the inclusion of Vietnam within the TPP.

Four Congresses in a row I have gotten passed in the House the Vietnam Human Rights Act. It has died in the Senate each time, sadly. It may get passed this year—who knows? But we know that even the State Department's book on trafficking just came out on Friday that Vietnam is a major source of labor trafficking and many products are made with child labor in Vietnam.

And yet they will now, if this treaty goes through on fast track, be in a situation where they will displace many of the textile capabilities of the Central American countries and put them out of business.

When you have forced labor, those dirt cheap wages, if there are wages at all, certainly makes the competitive advantage go toward Vietnam.

Is that being considered with the TPP or are you guys, for example, in the Western Hemisphere saying time out, Vietnam is an abuser, this will hurt Central America and will hurt El Salvador in an extremely—in an extreme way, and I think that is—we have got to put that on the radar.

So if you could speak to that as well, and I thank the chair for yielding time and if they could answer those questions I would deeply appreciate it.

Mr. SALMON. You know what? Go ahead. Take your time and answer those questions. This is the last question, and then we will close after that. So no problem.

Mr. PALMIERI. With regard to the screening processes of the children who are arriving, my understanding is that the Health and Human Services Department has the primary responsibility and would have the best information.

We do understand that there is both psychological and medical screening of all these children when they arrive, and that there is background checks done on who these children are being turned over to once they are processed through. The HHS——

Mr. SMITH. But how do you do a background check? Is it——

Mr. PALMIERI. I would say we would have to get back to you with a more specific answer——

Mr. SMITH. If you could get back with more specifics on that I would appreciate it.

Mr. PALMIERI [continuing]. From the Health and Human Services Department. I think your comments about the potential impact of TPP on Central America is something that we are all watching closely in the Western Hemisphere, in particular those governments themselves.

The trade representative have given us good information that TPP should not have a direct negative impact as the CAFTA–DR benefits should allow these countries to continue their access to our market even after TPP is moved forward. And I think that is——

Mr. SMITH. Because of tropical diseases perhaps USAID wanted to get this.

Mr. LOPES. Sure. Thank you, Congressman. First of all, thank you for your comments about USAID and their response, and thank you for your leadership on this issue.

In 4 years in this job it is the first time that neglected tropical diseases has come up in a direct briefing or hearing that I have participated in, and I know that those issues are very real for a lot of people.

It is part of our effort to continue with a broad base of programs—environment, health, agriculture—that are sort of all woven in to the root causes of opportunity. Health—if people can't sort of get through the basic health the first 5 years of their life they are certainly not going to be able to be positioned well to have opportunities and the ability to have an economic well being, which we have heard from our initial assessments, trying to understand why people are getting on these buses and trains—that, you know, certainly, that is one of the causes they have referenced.

We have limited health programs in the region compared to, say, 5 years ago in Latin America. We do have grants through the Pan American Health Organization and we do have some limited engagement on neglected tropical diseases. I can't speak specifically to hookworm or roundworm but we are happy to get back——

Mr. SMITH. Is that something you could ask—also ask HHS or whoever is administering the program who is on the ground? Because if they are not looking for it, again, co-morbidity is very high and these kids are walking with worms. Rather than feed the future we are feeding the worms and I know, you know, you understand that.

But if it is not being done as they come across the border this is a golden opportunity, one of the good positive outcomes that come from this mass influx, is to screen these kids and get them the deworming drugs to improve their lives.

Mr. SALMON. If I could interject, I went and visited the facility in Nogales where there is 1,250 children. So Representative Smith, there is 140 CBP officers working to care for these children and then there are FEMA representatives and there are HHS people there and they are doing health screenings for every child that is there.

Now, I don't know about the specifics of the worm issue but I know that the health of these children is a prime focus of our personnel that are on the ground working with these children.

In fact, one of the young teenagers that was there actually had a baby. Now, she didn't have it there in the facility. They took her to the local hospital in Nogales. But I saw her in one of the facilities with the baby by her side. And so——

Mr. SMITH. I appreciate that, and I appreciate your work on NTDs as well—a leader in the Congress. But if that is something you could check with them—if they are not looking perhaps to look to provide some healthier outcomes for these children.

Mr. LOPES. Yes. Certainly, I will get——

Mr. SMITH. I appreciate it. And on the trafficking real quick, hopefully the interagency council headed up by Luis CdeBaca is deploying very knowledgeable people to hopefully catch this working with law enforcement, of course, because it has gone under—right under our nose—two of my cities, major busts.

I will never forget when Chris Christie was U.S. Attorney. Remember that? Albio Sires will remember this. A bedroom community, whole group of Mexican minors found having been trafficked.

He busted up that ring and thankfully repatriated the young girls with their parents and families. But it could be going on in a very, very dangerous and robust way, if we are not careful, under the guise of this influx of children.

Mr. DUNCAN. Will the gentleman yield?

Mr. SMITH. Yes.

Mr. DUNCAN. I just want to say for the record, Mr. Chairman, there is not a single person on this dais or on this committee or in this Congress that is not very sympathetic to the humanitarian challenge that we have down there concerned about the children.

Oftentimes our comments are taken—when we focus on the border we focus on immigration reform, we focus on security and national security issues and what not. But we are very concerned about the children, and we want to make sure they are cared for.

We want to make sure they are reunited with their parents, hopefully in their home country, so they can return back to a normal way of life in their country and don't put a strain on the American resources.

But I think that is lost in the debate a lot of times that we are not concerned about children and absolutely we are. And so with that, I appreciate the gentleman yielding.

Mr. SALMON. And I am going to go ahead and just provide closing statements, and I am going to kind of segue from what you just said because it is about our border. It is about security.

But more than anything, the thing that kind of trumps them all is that the current policy is not compassionate. It is not, because for every child that ends up in one of these facilities and then is in the United States for 7 years waiting for a hearing because of some of our laws and we need to change those—we do—a child didn't make it.

The child may have died in the desert. The child may have been killed. That child may have been sold into slavery. And so what we are doing now is not compassionate, it is not smart and is not good policy.

And so we need to make sure that we send a clear message to those countries that if they pay $5,000 to $8,000 to get their child to America to get a free pass it is not going to be fruitful.

They won't get a free pass. Then they won't be spending that money anymore with these coyotes to get that done. They just won't. It will be a deterrent.

And so it is in all of our interests, on both sides of the aisle, to get that done and make sure that these children are back with their families in that loving environment.

So that having been said, this subcommittee is adjourned.

[Whereupon, at 3:22 p.m., the subcommittee was adjourned.]

APPENDIX

MATERIAL SUBMITTED FOR THE RECORD

SUBCOMMITTEE HEARING NOTICE
COMMITTEE ON FOREIGN AFFAIRS
U.S. HOUSE OF REPRESENTATIVES
WASHINGTON, DC 20515-6128

Subcommittee on the Western Hemisphere
Matt Salmon (R-AZ), Chairman

June 24, 2014

TO: MEMBERS OF THE COMMITTEE ON FOREIGN AFFAIRS

You are respectfully requested to attend an OPEN hearing of the Committee on Foreign Affairs, to be held by the Subcommittee on the Western Hemisphere in Room 2255 of the Rayburn House Office Building (and available live on the Committee website at http://www.ForeignAffairs.house.gov):

DATE: Wednesday, June 25, 2014

TIME: 2:00 p.m.

SUBJECT: Children Migrating from Central America: Solving a Humanitarian Crisis

WITNESSES: Mr. Francisco Palmieri
                   Deputy Assistant Secretary for Central America and the Caribbean
                   Bureau of Western Hemisphere Affairs
                   U.S. Department of State

                   Mr. Mark Lopes
                   Deputy Assistant Administrator
                   Bureau for Latin America and the Caribbean
                   U.S. Agency for International Development

By Direction of the Chairman

The Committee on Foreign Affairs seeks to make its facilities accessible to persons with disabilities. If you are in need of special accommodations, please call 202/225-5021 at least four business days in advance of the event, whenever practicable. Questions with regard to special accommodations in general (including availability of Committee materials in alternative formats and assistive listening devices) may be directed to the Committee.

COMMITTEE ON FOREIGN AFFAIRS

MINUTES OF SUBCOMMITTEE ON _____ *the Western Hemisphere* _____ HEARING

Day___ *Wednesday*___ Date_____ *06-25-2014*_____ Room___ *2255 RHOB*___

Starting Time ___ *2:00 p.m.*___ Ending Time ___ *3:22 p.m.*___

Recesses _____ (____to ____) (____to ____) (____to ____) (____to ____) (____to ____) (____to ____)

Presiding Member(s)

Chairman Matt Salmon and Rep. Jeff Duncan

Check all of the following that apply:

Open Session ☑   Electronically Recorded (taped) ☑
Executive (closed) Session ☐   Stenographic Record ☑
Televised ☑

TITLE OF HEARING:

"Children Migrating from Central America: Solving a Humanitarian Crisis"

SUBCOMMITTEE MEMBERS PRESENT:

Chairman Matt Salmon, Rep. Chris Smith, Rep. Jeff Duncan, Rep. Sean Duffy, Ranking Member Albio Sires, and Gregory Meeks.

NON-SUBCOMMITTEE MEMBERS PRESENT: *(Mark with an * if they are not members of full committee.)*

Ranking Member Eliot Engel and Rep. Joaquin Castro.

HEARING WITNESSES: Same as meeting notice attached? Yes ☑ No ☐
(If "no", please list below and include title, agency, department, or organization.)

STATEMENTS FOR THE RECORD: *(List any statements submitted for the record.)*

N/A

TIME SCHEDULED TO RECONVENE _____
or
TIME ADJOURNED ___ *3:22 p.m.*___

Subcommittee Staff Director